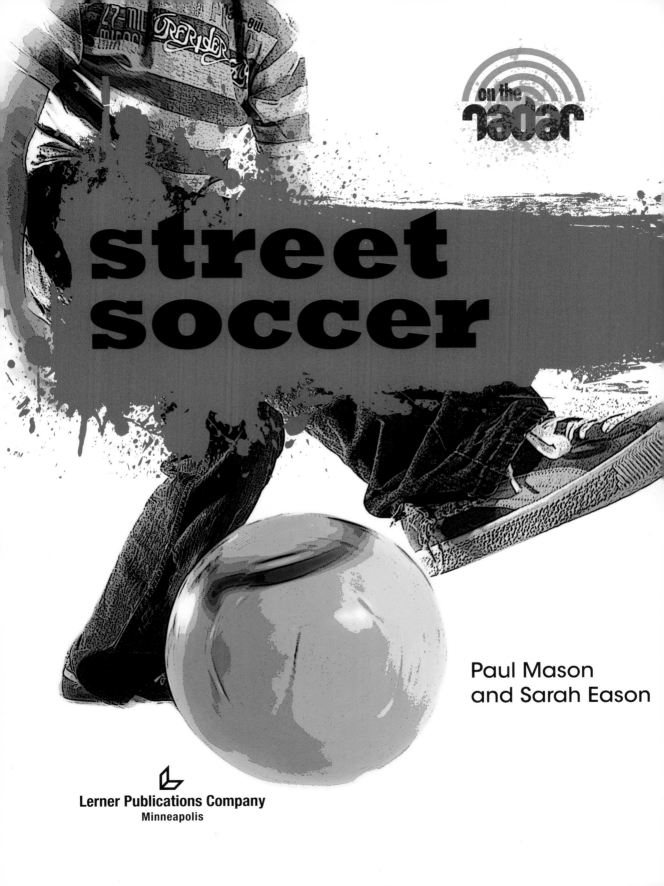

street soccer

Paul Mason
and Sarah Eason

Lerner Publications Company
Minneapolis

cover stories

First American edition published in 2012
by Lerner Publishing Group, Inc. Published
by arrangement with Wayland, a division
of Hachette Children's Books

Copyright © 2011 by Wayland

Lerner Publications Company
A division of Lerner Publishing Group, Inc.
241 First Avenue North
Minneapolis, MN U.S.A.

Website address: www.lernerbooks.com

Library of Congress Cataloging-in-Publication Data

Mason, Paul, 1967–
    Street soccer / By Paul Mason and Sarah
  Eason.
       p.   cm. — (On the radar: sports)
    Includes index.
    ISBN 978–0–7613–7760–3 (lib. bdg. : alk. paper)
    1. Soccer–Juvenile literature. I. Eason, Sarah.
  II. Title.
  GV943.25.M29 2012
  796.334—dc22   2011000466

Manufactured in the United States of America
  – CG – 7/15/11

Photo Acknowledgments
Images in this book are used with the
permission of: International Street Soccer
Association 2–3, 26b; Nelson de Kok/Ruud
Bos 24; Rex Features: Canadian Press 16–17;
Shutterstock: Aniad 25, Alex Jackson 1, Jan
Kranendonk 2r, 2t, 7, 30–31, Magicinfoto 4–5;
Kim Tamburri 13.

Main body text set in
Helvetica Neue LT Std 13/15.5.
Typeface provided by Adobe Systems.

30
TOP FIVE
Check out five of the best
street soccer games.

18
FIVE-MINUTE INTERVIEW
On the Radar talks to street soccer
expert Darren Laver.

6
WHY DO IT?
Find out the buzz
about street soccer!

22
BLOG SPOT
Read about a week in the life of a
professional street soccer player.

thepeople

12 **REAL-LIFE STORY** Live for soccer

16 **POSTER PAGE** Cristiano Ronaldo

18 **FIVE-MINUTE INTERVIEW** Darren Laver

22 **BLOG SPOT** Sean Thompson

24 **STAR STORY** Nelson & Ruud

themoves

8 **ZONE IN** The moves

10 **SHOW ME** The akka

14 **SHOW ME** Akka 3000

26 **ZONE IN** Freestyle moves

28 **SHOW ME** Spin the world

30 **TOP FIVE** The games

thetalk

4 **ALL ABOUT** Street soccer

6 **WHY DO IT?** The beautiful game

20 **THE LINGO** Street speak

32 **FAN CLUB** Get more info

32 **INDEX**

STREET SOCCER

Street soccer is fast, fierce, creative, and groundbreaking. It is a style of soccer that has come from the "street"—where players perform amazing acrobatic moves with the ball to outwit an opponent.

WHAT'S DIFFERENT?

Street soccer is all about using creative moves to control a ball within a street soccer game. Unlike regular team soccer, which has just one game and one set of rules, street soccer has lots of games, and each has its own rules or scoring system. Street soccer players attempt to outplay their opponents with fresh, creative, jaw-dropping moves. Many of the skills performed by street soccer players would not be allowed in a regular soccer game.

FROM THE STREET

Street soccer began on the streets of Amsterdam in the Netherlands. Players broke away from traditional soccer and started to invent their own new and creative style of soccer. The young soccer players juggled the ball in new and inventive ways—often never seen before. Their impressive moves caught on throughout the Netherlands and are spreading across the world.

What is freestyle soccer?

Street soccer players perfect their control of the ball by juggling it with their body, arms, legs, feet, and even their heads. This is called freestyle soccer.

Street soccer players practice freestyle moves to improve both their control of the ball and the moves they use within a street soccer game.

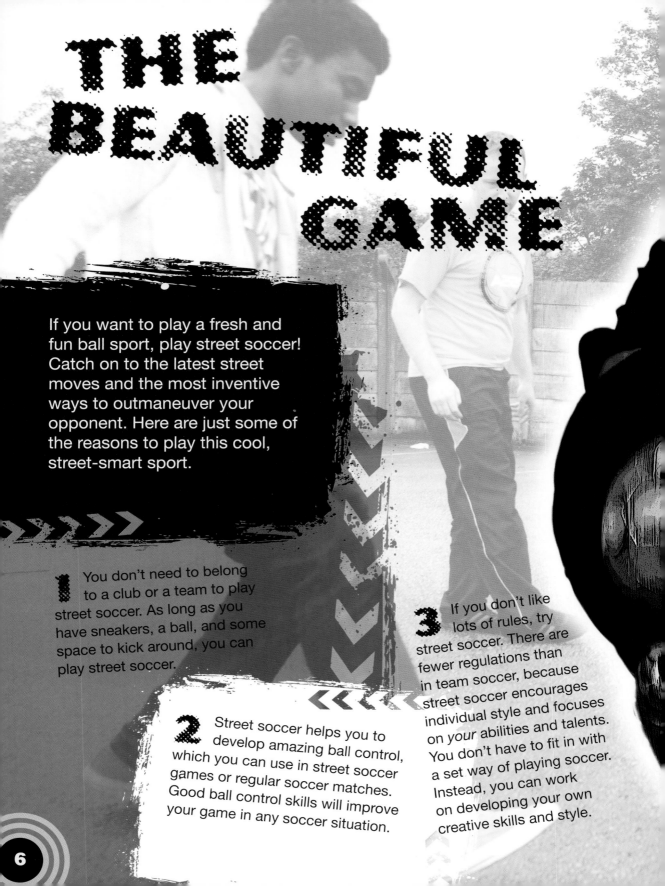

THE BEAUTIFUL GAME

If you want to play a fresh and fun ball sport, play street soccer! Catch on to the latest street moves and the most inventive ways to outmaneuver your opponent. Here are just some of the reasons to play this cool, street-smart sport.

1 You don't need to belong to a club or a team to play street soccer. As long as you have sneakers, a ball, and some space to kick around, you can play street soccer.

2 Street soccer helps you to develop amazing ball control, which you can use in street soccer games or regular soccer matches. Good ball control skills will improve your game in any soccer situation.

3 If you don't like lots of rules, try street soccer. There are fewer regulations than in team soccer, because street soccer encourages individual style and focuses on *your* abilities and talents. You don't have to fit in with a set way of playing soccer. Instead, you can work on developing your own creative skills and style.

4 If you become really good at street soccer and come up with an amazing move, it could even be named after you! Most of the great street soccer players have invented moves that now carry their name. The de Ruud move is named after Ruud Bos. Street soccer legend Issy "Hitman" Hamdaoui created the Issy Akka. Having a soccer move named after you is the ultimate street soccer mark of respect.

5 Street soccer is more than just a way of playing soccer. These days, it's a whole culture. Street soccer players call their culture *stilo*, meaning "style." You can tap into street soccer music, language, and clothing.

Street soccer is clever, creative, dynamic, and street smart. It's soccer with a built-in wow factor. Who wouldn't want to play it?

THE MOVES

The exciting moves performed by street soccer players aren't just designed to impress a crowd. They are used to outwit an opponent in a street game. To street soccer players, the moves shown here are just the basics. To most people, they are highly impressive!

AKKA

The player rolls the foot over the ball, moving it from side to side. This confuses the opponent into believing the ball will move in a certain direction so the player can move it in the opposite direction and out of reach.

THE FLICK

The player flicks the ball up and to the opponent's side. Then the player kicks the ball behind the opponent and runs past to collect it.

KNEE AKKA

In this move, the ball is flicked off the ground with the foot then hit with the outside of the knee. The player uses the foot to flick the ball away from the opponent.

AKKA 3000

This is another move used to keep control of the ball. The player flicks the ball up to waist height and spins 180 degrees to face the opponent. The player then uses a knee akka to flick the ball away from the opponent.

akka

the flick

akka 3000

knee akka

THE AKKA

Use the akka to outwit your opponent and to keep control of the ball.

You will need:

- soccer ball • sneakers
- space to practice

1

Start about a 3 feet (1 meter) away from your opponent. This will give you enough room to perform the move.

2

Move the ball to one side with the outside part of your foot.

3 Push the ball far in the opposite direction with the inside of the same foot.

4 Just before losing control of the ball, use the other foot to bring the ball back toward you and past the opponent.

Got it?

As the opponent moves in the fake direction of the ball, you can quickly move the ball out of reach!

LIVE FOR SOCCER

CHRISTINE TAMBURRI'S STORY

About two years ago, I was beginning to find team soccer really boring. The coaches were always shouting at us, and everyone had to play the same way. Even though I really loved soccer, it felt like all the fun was being sucked out of it.

Then I started playing street soccer. It was completely different. My regular soccer coach encouraged me to try out brand-new techniques and skills and to play soccer the way *I* wanted to. Eventually, my skills improved, and when I got to use them in matches, it only made me want to practice more!

After that I started searching the Internet for new moves. I practiced street moves all the time, and I kept on looking for new ways to improve my game. I didn't do it to win medals or trophies. I did it just because I loved the game.

Learning complex moves like the akka 3000 was a real breakthrough for me and a major achievement. Street soccer has given me a lot of satisfaction, and I've gotten a *lot* of respect from my friends too. These days, I don't just play street soccer—I live it!

AKKA 3000

You can use the akka 3000 for passing and shooting or getting past an opponent.

You will need:

• soccer ball • sneakers
• space to practice

1 Set up so that the opponent is to the right of you.

2 Use the foot to flick the ball up into the air to waist height.

3 Swivel around in a full circle as the ball rises up in the air.

4

Bring the leg up in a similar fashion to the knee akka (page 8) as you turn. Tap the ball with the knee, up into the air and away from the opponent.

5

Use the foot to kick the ball around the opponent.

Got it?

The opponent will move after the ball as you perform the first three steps of the move. The twist in step 4 allows you to then swivel away from the opponent and move the ball in another direction!

CRISTIANO RONALDO

THE STATS

Name: Cristiano Ronaldo
Born: February 5, 1985
Place of birth: Madeira, Portugal
Nationality: Portuguese
Job: Professional soccer player

GROWING UP

Cristiano grew up on the small island of Madeira off the coast of northwestern Africa. He started playing soccer on the island's dusty back streets and quickly grew into a brilliant performer. By the time he was 12 years old, Cristiano was the best soccer player on the island.

SPOTTED!

Cristiano began to play for Sporting Clube du Portugal. His exceptional skills were quickly spotted by leading clubs, such as England's Liverpool and Italy's Juventus. In 2003 the English club Manchester United signed Christiano when he was just 18 years old—for a staggering $19 million! It was the biggest amount of money ever paid by a club for a teenage soccer player.

FROM STREET TO STAR

In 2009 Cristiano was named FIFA World Player of the Year. In the same year, Manchester United traded him to Spanish soccer club Real Madrid for an incredible $127 million! Cristiano is the most expensive and most highly paid professional soccer player in the world.

ON THE STREET

Cristiano perfected his awesome football skills on the streets of Madeira. He claims that the best—and most creative—players come from the street. He regularly showcases his stunning street style on the professional field, showing off street soccer moves or impressive freestyle juggling skills.

DARREN LAVER

Street soccer coach Darren Laver is passionate about his game and teaches it all over the world. On the Radar thinks there's nothing Darren doesn't know about street soccer—so we put him to the test.

What is the best way for a beginner to get into street soccer?

The best way is to find a coach who can teach you core street soccer skills.

What equipment do you need to play street soccer?

That's the great thing about street soccer—all you need is a pair of sneakers and a ball. Almost anything can be used as goal markers—bags and clothing are the most popular. That's the beauty of the sport, you can set up and just play almost anywhere!

Where can you play street soccer?

You don't need a regular field to play street soccer. All you need is some space, such as a park or a yard. As long as your environment is spacious and safe, you can play street soccer there.

Is street soccer more dangerous than regular soccer?

Street soccer is probably less dangerous. In street soccer, you play creatively to outwit your opponent. Team soccer focuses more on aggressive tackling, in which players are more likely to be injured.

Can you use street skills in regular soccer?

Not all street soccer moves can be used in regular soccer matches, but moves such as the akka and the flick are used by players like Ronaldo all the time in professional games.

Do you use stilo in street soccer coaching sessions?

I play street soccer music during our coaching sessions. Using stilo music is a great way to pump up the creative atmosphere in a session. It gets players into the zone and really improves their creativity and skills with the ball.

STREET SPEAK

Get your stilo up to speed with this easy street speak guide.

drag
to slide the ball backward and forward in front of your opponent so that the opponent is thrown off balance

klapper
to make the ball move very quickly just by using the soles of the feet

search
to move the ball so that the opponent is forced to turn in a full circle

send
to use a trick move to send your opponent in the wrong direction

shock
to make the opponent flinch by pretending to kick the ball toward the opponent

annap
panna spelled backward. In this move, the player places the ball between the opponent's legs but from *behind* the opponent—so the move is a backward panna.

vanish
to make the ball disappear from the opponent's sight, such as by rolling the ball behind you or even hiding it inside your shirt!

GLOSSARY

Your guide to some of the
words used in the book

aggressive
fierce or rough

animated
made into a moving picture

forfeit
to give up something

groundbreaking
new and never seen before

immortalize
to earn lasting fame

orbit
to make a complete circle
around something

outmaneuver
to move more efficiently
than someone else. If you
outmaneuver an opponent
in street soccer, you move
the ball away from your
opponent and out of reach.

outwit
to be better than an opponent

panna
placing the ball between
your opponent's legs

**promo
(promotional
event)**
a gathering in which
something is brought to the
attention of many people

rotation
a circular movement

stilo
the word street soccer
players use to describe
street soccer culture

tricks
street soccer moves

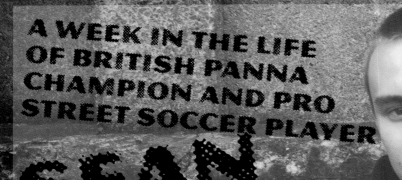

A WEEK IN THE LIFE OF BRITISH PANNA CHAMPION AND PRO STREET SOCCER PLAYER

SEAN THOMPSON

blog   **news**   **events**

SUNDAY

I was so tired this morning! I was up really early yesterday to go to a street soccer promo event. We were really on our game and did lots of freestyle moves. The crowd went crazy!

MONDAY

I watched a bit of *Rule of the Street* (a street soccer DVD) for some inspiration, then went to the local park for some freestyle juggling. I'm always trying to come up with new tricks, and I think I have a few in the making.

TUESDAY

I rolled out of bed at about 7:30 a.m., had a quick shower, and got dressed before my boss picked me up. At work I managed to pin down a booking for a street soccer show at an upcoming Adidas promo event. When I got home,

blog   news   events

I put on some Eminem and did some akkas and head balances to get ready for the event.

WEDNESDAY

We taught at an after-school club today, helping the kids work on basic akkas. Some of them are doing really well. After some warm-ups, we played life in a bottle, a cool game where players aim to knock over bottles filled with water.

THURSDAY

Today we headed to the Adidas event. I spent the morning setting up the stage. Then I had some time to kill, so I practiced my akka 3000. I practice whenever I can.

FRIDAY

I had a busy day at work today preparing for tomorrow's show at Manchester United. We have been asked to do a freestyle show at a club event. Lots of the best players are going to be there. So it's more important than ever that we perform well.

SATURDAY

I spent the morning at the Manchester United field making sure the music, lighting, and stage for the show tonight would all be OK. The show was great! Nobody made any mistakes. Result!

NELSON & RUUD

THE STATS

Name: Nelson de Kok
Born: August 22, 1986
Place of birth: Goirle, Netherlands
Job: Professional street soccer player

THE STATS

Name: Ruud Bos
Born: May 14, 1983
Place of birth: Oss, Netherlands
Job: Professional street soccer player

Nelson de Kok

Ruud Bos

NELSON FINDS FREESTYLE

As a child, Nelson lived, breathed, and slept soccer. As a teenager, he discovered freestyle soccer—and never looked back. Nelson's freestyle skills were exceptional, and in 2003, he wowed crowds with his impressive moves at the Masters of the Game freestyle soccer championships in Amsterdam. Almost as impressive as his freestyle moves was Nelson's age. He was just 17 years old and one of the youngest players to ever take part in the competition.

RUUD AND STREET

Ruud started playing soccer when he was only five years old. As he grew up, he became more and more interested in mastering complex soccer moves. His amazing freestyle skills marked him as an outstanding player. Shortly after appearing in the Masters of the Game tournament in Amsterdam, he was invited to work alongside Nelson on the *FIFA Street* computer game.

GAMEBOY HEROES

In 2004 the two players starred together in *FIFA Street*. The game immortalized them as true street soccer superheroes. The electrifying animated duo performed outstanding street soccer moves on-screen, making the game a huge international success. It also catapulted the two young sportsmen into street soccer stardom.

RULING THE STREET

In 2006 Nelson and Ruud followed their success in *FIFA Street* with two DVDs, *Rule of the Street* and *Soccer Kings*. *Soccer Kings* is a how-to DVD in which the street soccer super-team teach cutting-edge stunts and moves. *Rule of the Street* showcases these two players as well as their freestyle soccer skills.

TOP OF THEIR GAME

Nelson and Ruud are recognized as two of the world's hottest street soccer stars. They regularly showcase street soccer moves on TV; support workshops for young, up-and-coming street players; and are in demand from leading sports companies for their advertising power. When it comes to soccer, Nelson and Ruud rule!

FREESTYLE MOVES

neck balance

soles of the feet

Freestyle moves are used by street soccer players to improve their ball control skills. If a player can control the ball, that player can control the game—and win!

spin the world

NECK BALANCE

The ball is thrown up gently. As the ball comes down, the player moves the head down and forward, and cushions the ball on the back of the neck. The player may bring the arms out to the side to stop the ball from rolling off.

SOLES OF THE FEET

The player lies on the back and throws the ball up above the chest. The player brings up one foot and balances the ball on the sole. Then the player puts both legs in the air and juggles the ball between the feet.

SPIN THE WORLD

The player goes into a neck balance, then brings the arms forward and hands together. The player nudges the ball to one side and spins it toward the arms. The ball is rotated around the arms and back to the neck.

HEAD BALANCE

The player throws the ball onto the forehead while leaning back. The player moves the feet from side to side to help balance the ball.

head balance

27

SPIN THE WORLD

This freestyle juggling move allows you to control the ball with the neck, the chest, and the arms. The trick is to make the ball do a full orbit of the head, using the arms as a track.

You will need:

- soccer ball
- space to practice
- patience!

1

Use a neck balance move to balance the ball at the base of the neck, with the head tilted forward. Stretch the arms out in front of you and hold your hands.

2

Rotate the body counterclockwise. Move the ball to the left of the head, between the ear and the crook of the elbow.

Keep turning the body so that the ball moves to the front of the head. It should rest between the hands and the head.

3

4

Continue to turn counterclockwise until the ball reaches a point between the right ear and the right elbow. Then let it return to its starting place at the back of the head.

Got it?

The ball should have made one full rotation around the head. Keep practicing the move until you can send the ball around the head twice—without stopping!

THE GAMES

Street soccer games are exciting, fast-paced displays of freestyle magic. Unlike regular soccer, street soccer games can be played with a handful of players (some with just two). Here are some of the best street soccer games:

1. 3 V 3 SWITCH

Six soccer players play, with three players in each team (3 v 3). The size and type of ball used to play the game is changed (or switched) every minute. Lots of different balls are used, from tennis balls and soccer balls to footballs. The aim is for players to score as many goals as they can in two minutes. Game on!

2. 3 V 3 MINES

Six players play this game, with three players in each team. Two balls are used. One ball is the mine and is placed on a cone in the middle of the playing area. The other ball is the soccer ball. Players aim to score as many goals in the opposition's net as they can without knocking the mine off the cone as they play. If a player does knock off the mine, the player's team must do a forfeit—chosen by the other team!

3. 1 V 1 PANNA

There are two players in this game. Each tries to "out-panna" the other player. The player who scores the most pannas—gets the ball through the opponent's legs the most times—in two minutes wins.

4. 3 V 3 PANNA FREEZE

In panna freeze, six players play, with three players on each team. The aim is to score as many goals against the opposition as possible. The twist is that if a player is "panna-ed" (an opponent kicks the ball through the player's legs), he or she must freeze for 20 seconds before continuing to play!

5. LIFE IN A BOTTLE

This is a game in which, instead of goals, each team has two open plastic bottles filled with water. Six players play, with three on each team. Players aim the ball at the other team's bottle. The aim is to knock over the opponent's bottle, spilling the water inside. The defender has to quickly pick up the bottle to avoid losing water. After three minutes, the team with the most water in its bottle wins.

31

GET MORE INFO

Books & DVDs

Contro, Arturo. *Cristiano Ronaldo*. New York: Rosen Publishing, 2008. Read a biography about the Portuguese superstar who uses street soccer moves in his pro game.

D'Arcy, Sean. *Freestyle Soccer Street Moves and Tricks*. Richmond Hill, ON: Firefly Books, 2009. Professional freestyler Sean D'Arcy teaches some of his favorite tricks in this book.

Soccer Kings: Air Moves. Amsterdam: Destiny Bound Entertainment, 2006. Five world-class street soccer players show basic techniques through advanced air moves in this DVD.

Soccer Kings: Ground Moves. Amsterdam: Destiny Bound Entertainment, 2006. Five of the world's best street soccer players teamed up to show some of the sport's best ground moves.

Websites

Freestyle Soccer
http://www.freestylesoccer.ca/
This website focuses on freestyle soccer in North America.

Nelson de Kok
http://www.nelsondekok.com/site/en/index.htm
Visit Nelson de Kok's website to find out what he's been doing.

Ruud Bos
http://www.ruud7bos.com/
Ruud Bos's website has links to other sites, including de Kok's, and a picture gallery.

INDEX

ball control, 5, 6, 8, 10, 27, 28
Bos, Ruud, 7, 24–25
coaches, 12, 18
equipment, 6, 18, 30–31
FIFA Street, 25
freestyle soccer, 5, 17, 25, 26–27, 28–29

games, 5, 6, 19, 23, 30–31
Hamdaoui, Issy, 7
Kok, Nelson de, 24–25
Masters of the Game, 25
moves, freestyle soccer, 5, 22, 25, 28–29
moves, street soccer, 7, 8–9, 10–11, 12, 14–15, 17, 19, 23, 25, 28–29

Netherlands, 4, 24–25
regular soccer, 4, 6, 18–19
Ronaldo, Cristiano, 16–17, 18
Rule of the Street, 22, 25
Soccer Kings, 25